pendulum

pendulum

Poems by
Eric Scott Sutherland

Accents Publishing • Lexington, Kentucky • 2014

Printed in the United States of America

Accents Publishing
Editor: Katerina Stoykova-Klemer
Cover Photo: Vladislav Hristov
Cover Design: Simeon Kondev

Library of Congress Control Number: 2014938762
ISBN: 978-1-936628-25-4
First Edition

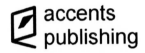

Accents Publishing is an independent press for brilliant voices. For a catalog of current and upcoming titles, please visit us on the Web at

www.accents-publishing.com

Contents

Then it was as if I suddenly saw the secret beauty of their hearts, the depths of their hearts, where neither sin nor desire nor self-knowledge can reach, the core of their reality, the person that each one is in God's eyes. If only they could all see themselves as they really are. If only we could see each other that way all the time.

—Thomas Merton, from *Conjectures of a Guilty Bystander*

the gate

Enter by the narrow gate. For the gate is wide and the way is easy
that leads to destruction, and those who enter by it are many.
For the gate is narrow and the way is hard that leads to life,
and those who find it are few.

Matthew 7:13–14

The gate is iron,
a twin set of towering black spears
attached in rows, stretched between limestone
pillars, married by a diagonal of chain links
and steel knots tied with padlocks.
Two dark wings etched into the entrance
cut into blacktop when swinging wide to visitors.
Before opening, the eager press their faces
between the bars, impatient
with the wait to unlock the gate.
If they could slim to snakes
and slither on in, they would
find the Gatekeeper turning on the few
lights illuminating his small corner
counting down the hours until he could slip
out through the narrow back door
invisible to the raving horde.

you find yourself

here in Central—
the belly button of a town,
the center point where all
spokes of the community
wheel converge. A few
limp skyscrapers lean over
a weave of parking lots, historic
remnants and neighborhoods
in various stages of bloom
and decay. In a dim rotunda,

a

                    pendulum

    sways

(and sometimes stops).

It is a library, it is a chess
board, it is a skull full
of keys, it is a city
park, a theater
stage, it is a crime
scene, and it is a purgatory,
a battleground between light
and dark. Have and have-not
make do with what remains.
The Gatekeeper observes
from a corner near the entrance.

Sleepwalker

Limping along in canvas
deck shoes, skinny beneath
an untucked Goodwill dress shirt
and a starched stiff pair
of three dollar stonewashed jeans,
he's a doppelganger
of a Spinal Tap member;
the good time lines etched
deep around squinting slits,
gouged into sagging cheeks,
shoulder length rock 'n' roll mullet
spiked every which way
like a rooster or a Rolling Stone.
Always coming and going,
a perpetual state
of sleepwalking,

                a purgatory
between opening and closing,
inhabits a lonely no man's land
dividing a shit-faced heaven
and a cold-sober hell.

Milkshake Ricky

loves oatmeal cookies
and peanut butter shakes,
dresses in cut-off sweats
over full-length
sweats, looks like he flew
out of the cuckoo's nest,
lost four pair of glasses
and two umbrellas
last week.

Milkshake Ricky is losing
more than his mind. The way
he fumbles through
layers of worn cotton
searching for his billfold
he may have also
lost what little
money there is left
from his monthly check.

the best, the best

he's from Cuba
the best music
we talk boxing
and baseball
the best, the best
I hand him a cup
of coffee and ask

so, why are you here?

the pendulum's rod
cuts twice through
the cloud of every
stranger's breath
a worn earth turns
another nth degree

we both smile
knowing the answer

plague

is always a dirty
paw away.

a hand not washed
in who knows how long.

a hand stained by soil
and cigarette resin, the filth
permanent under fingernails.

a hand sprouting long claws
the color of skin, camouflaged,
each one a hook, a tool to dig.

a hand counting out
eighty pennies for a soda.

how to keep from going out of business

y'all take stamps here?

man eats salt not pepper
from a tiny paper packet

you'd get more business if you did

the widow's mite

Mark 12:41–44 and Luke 21:1–4

Do I get credit
for bringing new customers?
the well-heeled woman
wants to know.
Not a single one
in her party leaves a tip.
Meanwhile, the unappointed
Mayor of Central Library,
in clothes as old as I am,
buys a large coffee,
hands over two worn
George Washingtons
and a quarter, says
You know what to do
with the change.

have and have-not

In the dim rotunda
two people sit,
inanimate as mannequins.

One is dressed in slate
a three-piece uniform.

The other wears a rainbow
of second-hand mismatches.

They watch a pendulum
swing beneath the eye of the sky,
marking the miserable
seconds of the day,
the tick-tocks of rat claws
as they race.

In one's wide dark
pupils, the dream is unattainable.

And in the other one's, the myth is
exposed, hope already lost.

when man returns to beast

it doesn't take much
to make a man wild again
like great great Papaw Neanderthal
let a season pass, every second spent
foraging for grub, man must hunt
will transform right on the streets
impossible not to revert to beast
when every single thought is
what am I going to eat?

possession

is a burden
you end up dragging
with you everywhere
you go

man of steel forearms

Shove your life
into Glad bags.

Clench hands
around each one.

This is the shape
of home,

as mobile as the legs
carrying it along.

Never let yourself
sit for too long.

fishing for change

lost skipper, Phoenix Park, far from sea
hair grayish green like rocky coast
moss tangled under an old sock hat
a body of wire wrapped in a ragged coat
shredded to stuffing and thread
an unlit cigarette hangs between thin lips
a ship tossed in the storm of his beard
every morning voyage passes the pay phone
he casts his finger into the coin return slot
but I have never seen him get lucky
never seen him catch a dime

the restless

Stoplight paints
wet pavement red.
It's after midnight
and the restless
still wander black roads.

Night hides hideous
wounds until daybreak
reveals them. The city
an infection, orange flame
devouring stars.

trickle down

Mornings after
nights spent
in a club where
women strip,
two dollar bills
stick to his fingertips
like magic tricks
gone haywire;
he grins
like a pedophile
in a crowd of kids
as he flicks
each one into the jar
marked *tips*.

Holly Hollow

she's loose
for how much she loses
as hard as daddy's fists
crimes never confessed

one quick glance
might confuse
dark tattoos
and purple bruises

learns about sex
prior to the little
curly hairs of puberty
before she chooses

one blue dyed bang
curled like a finger
beckons come here
I'll fuck you real good

silent siren

She holds her Mountain
Dew like a baby's bottle.
Hot pink hair shouts
like a house fire in the night
against the cool blue of her satin
Kentucky Wildcat jacket.
The scream of color does little
to light up her aura,
dim and gray as this building.

vengeance is a bastard

Bastard son blazes
with the gaze of a starving raptor,
stalks his biological father
not seen in twenty years.

Agent Orange

The
streets are
the safest refuge
since surviving Nam.
A sense of humor and homeless Zen
suggests a life not drafted, his youth not stolen
by the bloody talons of the War Goblin, his tent mate
not a vicious hunter stacking the heads of innocent villagers
between their green Army cots each Armageddon night in a gruesome
pyramid.

out, kicked out

I am a quiet fire
in the corner, the light
in the mirrored eye of the healer
where blanketing burdens
can be stripped bare.

I cannot tell
if he is blushing,
deep in thought
or just flustered under
purple eye shadow
and thick eyeliner.

He escaped with
a suitcase and piggy bank,
to the safety of a shelter.
No going home. No returning
to the boy whose pink cheeks
his mother loved to pinch.

His father threw the son
he could no longer love
a curve, out of the house,
disapproval still written
in cursive
cuts and bruises.

Reader, a question

Ever been so hungry
as to trade your
driver's license,
your dignity
for a day-old muffin,

something worse?

scratching posts

Onyx eyes dart off when lit
with my wordless inquisition.
She works hard to hide
what hurts, two pale forearms
striped with reddened welts,
like fleshy posts scratched by cats
visible beneath short sleeves.

With a razorblade,
a butter knife, a broken
piece of glass, uses any edge
that will tear the thin
paper of tender skin,
carving a signature on her
body, her masterpiece of pain.

Baby Baby

Someone's daughter
struts in butt hugging tights
and a tiny halter top,
shakes her blooming body,
just a baby on display
for drive-by viewing.

In a year, she's pushing
a handed-down stroller,
no *come here* sway
in her hips, the same
little girl with a baby
of her own.

Willie the Walrus

Willie Wittle, who
some call Buck,
but I named the Walrus,
pimps a zoot suit
with tennis shoes—
has seven of them,
one for every occasion:
two for church, two
for dances, three
for funerals and whatever
else comes up.
Problem is
he can't get his loafers
out of the Shoe Doc's shop.
He whines from the arc
in his horseshoe 'stache,
twists his forlorn face
into his trademark grimace,
counting out a dollar's worth of coin
for his favorite can of lemon-lime pop.
They want forty-three dollas!

Half-Hawk the Behemoth

> By judging others we blind ourselves to our own evil and
> to the grace which others are just as entitled to as we are.
>
> —Dietrich Bonhoeffer, *The Cost of Discipleship*

A bald behemoth with half a Mohawk
running down the back of his skull,
passes through the gate as if in slow
motion. The shadow cast
chills skin like an ill omen.

Eyebrows shaved, John Wayne
Gacy clown face, no makeup,
in military issue camouflage,
large green duffel stuffed full,
a snail's shell on his back,
a purple X on the side,
packs a fishing pole in his hand.

You are caught
holding your breath, waiting
for the scoop after "breaking news ..."
Kid killer turned loose? Or derelict defender
of orphans and other strays saves the day?

Henry Earl's James Brown blues

Henry Earl's kung fu-ed all the hooey
he can muster from feeble chops
and *get off the bad foot* kicks
dressed to the hilt
in secondhand threads
could be a seventies B-movie jive turkey
staggering yellow-eyed day and night
too alive to be called zombie
but certainly under the spell
of a Wild Irish Rose
liquid voodoo

he hangs on like hackberry
along fencerows, despite rumors
of tuberculosis and a schizophrenic
alcoholic constitution that insists
he is *the* James Brown
a record of more than one thousand
arrests—testament to his survival skills

at the end of another one man act
when he is tired and tore
transforms into a master of strategy—
waves his karate chop wand,
conjures the jailhouse,
a refuge from extremes
where he receives a free meal,
can lay his heavy head down
and try to dream another dream

GRRR

If you can crack
the shellac, penetrate her
vinyl veneer, see through
her sinister Goth facade,
a *GRRR* from that girl
is like a grin.

the hardness of soft bodies

Middle-aged men who know nothing
but a life of street hustling and holding it down
hard in a prison yard or public commons
soften to stay out of trouble,
their days are mazes of struggle,
rap and scat about *dem Cats.*

hush

the ones who do not speak
muffle my joy the most

lips too stitched
to spit out what hurts

occasionally one will nod
or surprise with the wave of a hand

always the loudest
sound of my day

Babel

an addict too fucked up
to tell the time or to know
whether it is Thursday or Friday
petitions every passing person
with his lunatic gibberish

steps (more than twelve)

Life
is
a
series
of
steps
a
zigzag
walking
path
sometimes
we
stumble
into
the
ditch
or turn ninety degrees
          and
          tumble
          off
          cliffs

but steps
nonetheless

regular American

The public I serve
too distracted to read the signs.
Got any regular American? The time?
Sand slips through a Styrofoam
cup, and I feel trapped,
in a rerun of despair,
a fly stuck behind a wall of glass
counting every speck of sand
in the hour, a smart phone
buried like a dark secret in Phoenix
Park. The bathroom is
on every floor but this one.
You can take the elevator or stairs.
Up or down. down or Up.
I don't have Mountain Dew
but I do have "A Late One."
It's early enough
the sun is still
yawning, up there
somewhere behind a veil
of clouds, up where
our whispered prayers go
to find whatever
we call god.

not in the job description

Librarians are almost always very helpful
and often almost absurdly knowledgeable.
Their skills are probably very underestimated
and largely underemployed.

—Charles Medawar

You went to school
to study library science,
to become an ambassador
for letters and literacy.
You love books
and want to help
people read.
You never expected
you'd spend most of your day
directing people to the bathroom
and repeating, *this is the library,*
you cannot fall asleep.

Speed King

sleep easy now, Speed King
reign complete, body conquered
heart ground up in the rib cage

the fire that drove you
to devour every hour
extinguished your flame

eyes

Their eyes
have learned
to look down,
turn away.

Their eyes
struggle to stay bright,
proud when dimmed
to beg.

Their eyes
scan every corner
for an advantage,
spare change.

Their eyes
are more adept
at counting arrests
than steps.

Their eyes
storm blood
red lightning
from liquid alibis.

Their eyes
are blackened
from convenient scrips
and lovers' fists.

Their eyes
wide, seeing daddy's

secret surprise at bedtime,
no lullabies.

Their eyes
find a safe place where
janitors and security guards
never sweep.

Their eyes
that cannot read
but can spell
r-a-p-e.

Bobby Black Nose

At 9 am, a cup
of coal colored Columbian
is the kick in the pants—
then off to his second floor hideout
for an ass pocket whiskey swig.

By noon, a cup
of soup and a couple of packs
of saltine crackers.
Bobby Black Nose
loves the chicken gumbo.

At 3 pm, drags his legs
up South Hill to Two
Keys where he leans
on the bar, alone.
He's in between

mo(u)rning and moonlight
shifts, Budweisers
and Heaven Hill shots,
misses the company
of someone besides the ghost.
Bobby Black Nose
can't put down the bottle.

By midnight, at Tolley Ho
scrambling eggs and frying
taters for frat boys.
Their jeers and whispers
find the kitchen, his ears.
His black nose, a dulled Rudolph,

like he took a punch
from an invisible fist.

Old Red Harris

retired professor,
silver-haired South Dakotan,
of ranches not reservations,
keeps the Gatekeeper in books.
A father figure in rant,
windbreaker, and ball cap
can spot a victim before the gun
fire, always threatened suicide
before he turned sixty-five,
now seventy-two
as steady as the morning
alarm, then one sunrise gone.

Old white Indian,
what river of tears
have you left behind
for those who survive
to discover?
Loved one, are you lost,
do you haunt black hills,
the home shared
with brothers burning red?
Do you run with the hunted?

There is unending
thunder in every heart
and holy land paleface stole.
The same face stares back
from history in the mirror,
drove you deep into the mute
corners of the mind,
the bedroom closet

where you drank to drown
the sound of growing old,
footsteps from long ago,
a whole world full of bullet holes.

dim rotunda

Do not let yourself enter,
the dome is shattered,
a single shaft of light appears
sick as it falls thin
through the chasm.
The world has stopped turning,
a frozen pendulum mutters.
The vacant have occupied all rooms.
There is no teacher here
to guide you, the poison
hemlock has been drunk,
the master's body
still, a granite statue.

questioning a suicide

for Robert Hundley-Doria

I thought you escaped
danger, the death trap
of battlefield, Bush's war
for oil. Back home,
you put on a security guard's outfit
instead of a soldier's uniform.
Handsome, compassionate,
quiet, I watched the ladies
gaze at you in admiration,
never noticed all the cracks
just beneath your all-American facade,
the warning siren in your silence.
It seemed the dull days full of vagrants
and the mundane carousel of ordinary
patrons had saved you,
a drunk with a stashed bottle
or a loon shadowboxing the pendulum,
no problem compared to an insurgent
with a bomb hidden beneath clothes.
Come Monday morning, opening,
shocked when I was told
your name added to the casualty list.

the definition of insanity

> places haunted
> Now with whatever it was we left there
> To find whatever it was we wanted.
>
> —Joe Bolton, from *Woodshedding: Kentucky, 1980*

There he is again
hiding hands
in empty pockets.
His jaw juts out
as an underbite, mouth
turned to permanent frown
like a horseshoe spilling its luck,
the weight pulling his head
toward the floor.

When he walks in
he immediately looks up
toward the glass top
of the rotunda,
five stories high,
where the world's
largest ceiling clock
keeps time
while he's busy
killing it, a pendulum.

He'll be back tomorrow
and the day after that
and the day
after that
and the
day
after that,

as if he expects
to see something new,
he might have missed,
some miraculous light
shining down
that wasn't there
the day before
or the day before
or the day before.

invisible city

Here it is Main
Street, the epicenter,
east-west ground zero,
its population multiplies
as spring temperatures
warm to summer swelter.
The limit as far
as the road reaches.

Eager fingers pierce
the softest pockets
imprisoned in the park
where everything is hard
clenched fists, cement facades.

Forgotten children,
overwhelmingly sons,
grown men with the wild vacancy
of wayward boys in their eyes,
lack the guidance of mothers.

You just know their souls
have been dug into by vulture
beaks and claws, the fanged
snouts of feral hounds who
prowl the streets looking to feast.

Expressions are explosions—crazy
crayon scribbles
across blank pages, defaced
and stained faces, frozen
in time at five, nine, fourteen.

Raggedy Annie and Little Miss Muppet

Raggedy Annie,
bruised and ghostly,
she wants rock candy,
raw sugar, little packets
of sweetness to soothe her
fidgety fix. And Little Miss
Muppet with two teeth left
to grit, cannot eat a muffin.
She is wasting away to a skeleton
but a small, shapely ass saves,
is the redeeming feature
in the minds of the cracked
who'd rather suck a glass dick.
Their gold-toothed pimp
only interested in selling
something to hump.

government check blues

government check
keeps young dopes
strung out and out
of work   broke
sitting in the park
all day, getting high
getting drunk

*panhandler's fib**

Sir
I
ran out
of gas, left
my billfold home, I
get paid at the end of the week.

* *Fib*—a new poetry form based on the Fibonacci sequence

the Gatekeeper

after six years as gatekeeper
to the asylum, the Samaritan in me

has become a cynic
I'm so sick

of wannabe pimps wasting
their youth on worn-out whores

madmen like caged animals
zigzagging the floors

nervous addicts twitching
in every corner for a new cleaner fix

of seeing that haunted hollow
expression on a battered woman's face

I'm about to hop
on the carousel as well

and completely
lose my shit

then, the seizure, an epiphany
the god-spark sizzling in them all

vitriolage

1

Tears fall in a downpour
and I yearn to restore her
life before the damage, reach
for the faucet distilling patience.

Her expression holds
the scream, emblazoned
in her melted face—

brownish pink like raw meat
marbled rye melanin

swirling skin resettled
into a new contour
for nose, lips, cheeks.

A tear trickles through
the scarred terrain.

2

It was Sunday morning
before church service
in the Greater Soul
Deliverance Tabernacle.

Vocal chords were being
warmed for hymns.

The soprano, embarrassed
by the choir leader
for singing off key, passed

the accusation like a collection
plate to her neighbor.

Like a copperhead tongue
unwound, the finger pointer
struck, a mad clap of thunder,
storm of acid, burning down.

3

The tiniest scent
of stress
is the catalyst.

She starts suddenly,
the shrill wheeze of a balloon,
pinched air rushing
to escape. Her mantra
rises with great momentum,
a tea kettle whistle
wailing when water
finally boils.

sorry sir, sorry
sir, sorry
sir, sorry sir
sorry sir, sorry
sir, sorry sir,
sorry

homicide detective

He looks like death,
eyes ringed black like a coon's—

the eyes of dead bodies, no sleep,
a Folgers IV and rolled gold leaf.

Unconcerned with who hears what,
while waiting for his ham to come up.

It squeals and pops, hot on the grill.
He cracks a quick joke

about getting rid of
a victim's pesky mother.

second chance

What are you going to do
when the door to the pen
is flung open?

Make your way
to a distant city
try to assume
a new anonymous life.

Another body in line
at the halfway house
not too proud to take
what is handed out.

At interviews dressed
as nice as one can
with lint in pocket.

How can you convince
the man who says no—yes
you are worth the risk
left your mistakes
behind prison bars?

How can you convey
all you really want
is a steady job?
All you really want—
a small apartment.

strange fruit

> Here is fruit for the crows to pluck,
> For the rain to gather, for the wind to suck,
> For the sun to rot, for the trees to drop,
> Here is a strange and bitter crop.

> —Dwayne P. Wiggins, Maurice Pearl and Lewis Allan
> from the Billie Holiday song *Strange Fruit*

At the corner of Woodland
and Old Vine, whether
the chill of February
or the melt of July,
she stands like a street
tree by the curb.

She is native but alien,
prominent against a backdrop
of brick and honeysuckle.
A full-length hooded parka
like synthetic gray bark
covers her small body,
head to ankle.

Her strange fruit—
plastic grocery bags
stuffed and tied in round balls—
spills on the sidewalk
under her limbs
like June apples
or Osage oranges.

status quo

blueberry is the apple
juice of the muffin
world in the universe
of bread and circus

will listen to sermon for food

I am not surprised
to find Jesus here
among the poor and damaged.
These are your people. True
believers packing their bibles
call out his name
more than the righteous
who claim their god resides
in vacuous stadium-sized churches.
Here, god is
embodied in the temple
of spirit, in people
who build faith
into architecture of action.

god bless you brother

But some are holy only
because they are hungry
and will sit patiently
while the preacher reassures
Jesus is lord and indeed
died for their sins.
They understand
that at the final amen
no matter how saintly or sinful
they will be served a free hot meal
the hollow beast eating them
from the inside out
for the time being, quieted.

a greater depression

Times are tough
as a calloused knuckle.

A woman scrounges
through a fair trade purse
searching for the treasure
to pay for her family's lunch,
her arm sunk to the elbow.

Eventually a nervous hand emerges
triumphant with three silver half dollars,
three Sacajaweas, and a Susan B—
the crumbs of their savings.

Nothing in the bowl but dust.

No manifesting destiny, but busted,
west of the hot Western world
where the hopeless multiply like a mob
outside the locked gate.

Hector

Hector, are you homesick?
In your hand, the brown paper sack
wrapped around a stack of aging pictures—
your grandchildren, the time you took a trip
to Paris, your home in Veracruz.

Hector, can't you hear me?
Over and over you have shown
the same sad slideshow
of snapshots in a ritual amnesia,
mornings just like this one
while waiting for your long espresso.

Hector, each time I tried
connecting, nodding recognition,
sending poor Spanish transmissions. You
stood so close on the other side
of the counter, sequestered
in the isolation of memory, somewhere
where you are always understood.

acceptance

Two thousand six hundred
miles of road from home,
his time split between
two jobs. Checks halved
with those left behind.
His biggest wish
being accepted
into the university.

Rolando from Guatemala
works six days a week,
and when I see him he smiles
wide and helps me speak
in his tongue.
Siempre la mismo.

When not washing dishes
in a mall garden of olives,
cashes in his time off
reading and studying English
to further understand
the empire's language.

pendulum

Mornings before the bus arrives,
Miss Emily is perched
on her front porch like a pigeon
in a purple and gray wad
of scarf, toboggan, and tattered jacket.

The shotgun where she sleeps
is in shambles and so is she, inching toward
death across the cold floor of the rotunda
where a five-story pendulum
marks this particular passage.

She shuffles along in toe lengths,
puckers up to suck
short breaths before speaking
in a weak, hushed tone,
hot ham 'n' cheese.

Wrinkles wrap tree
rings around her face.
Her scent more a stench,
so sweet and foul, the drugstore
perfume she wears cannot cover it.

Some mornings she forgets her coat
on the old swivel chair on the porch
and everyone who passes, sees.
Patiently, it waits for her return,
the pendulum swings.

On a day like any other
she leaves, and what remains
fades into the rot of the forgotten,

where the shotgun was demolished,
a newly planted garden.

the Saint of Selflessness, or SOS

There is no need
to huddle under a pine wing
in the park or tuck away
a rusty cage in an ashtray-toilet
corner in the parking garage
to make a bed.
He has a room rented,
a porch to sit on, and a metal
box with his name on it
to receive mail.

Once a teen
hustler who used
youthful lank and skinny
ass as commodity,
he never got further
into the story, but somewhere,
after his brother hung
dying way before his time,
he discovered Jesus,
the word in the good book;
how an unforgiving faith,
a belief in something greater
can keep you held together
when all else fails.

There is no reason
for him to be here
seven days a week,
skin and bone beacon
shining into darkness,
touching every bright

and bruised soul
with equal kindness,
but to many he is a buddy,
a cash advance, a spare
cigarette, a cup of coffee.
A kind of everyday savior.

Harley

When my ninety year old grandmother,
discouraged by her vanishing
vision, makes a living out of listing
all of the things she can no longer do,
I let his story unfurl
like a fern from my tongue.

Harley, a blind man
with no companion
or seeing dog to lead,
plays the keys, feels
the difference between
a five, a ten, a single,
tells jokes where he is
often the butt,
never orders lunch
without a piece of chocolate,
or allows the darkness to keep
him from beaming bright.

He maneuvers the city maze,
the well worn ruts of Central
with nothing but his joy
and a thin cane.
I tell her she is lucky
and we are all making do
with what remains.

All Saints

The morning after
Halloween, the nightmare

continues in broad daylight.
No masks to cover cracked faces,

clothes in layers, tatters.
No makeup for cuts and bruises,

dried crust of blood
and grime on the fingers.

All saints.

questioning a pendulum

Why not cease to swing
when your trajectory crosses
a position of equilibrium?

> Is this what we are supposed to glean
> from your hypnotic repetitive motion
> —that no destination finds balance?

Is it all about gravity,
revolution?

> Do you display for us, our active lives
> we have stilled, that the earth, you
> and everything contained within it
> keeps turning?

Are you another diversion,
as a shoestring to a curious cat?

> Or are you just a large finger
> marking with every pass
> each birth, each death?

About the Author

Eric Scott Sutherland is a hawk watcher, Kentucky creek walker, tree-loving Lorax, community and event organizer, the author of two chapbooks and the full-length collection, *incommunicado* (2007). *pendulum* is his fourth book of poems. He is the creator and host of Holler Poets Series, a monthly celebration of literature and music since 2008. Eric makes his nest in Lexington. Follow Eric and Holler at *ericscottsutherland.com*.

Acknowledgments

I'd like to thank Rebecca Gayle Howell for seeing the light in these poems in their infancy. This project might never have grown wings without her encouragement. Words cannot express my love and appreciation for my editor/publisher, Katerina Stoykova-Klemer. Her poetic friendship and guidance through this process has been and continues to be invaluable. I am so happy she called shotgun on this book! I appreciate Leigh Anne Hornfeldt, Kate Hatfield, Jude McPherson, Fielden Willmott, Mikey Swanberg, Jeremy Paden, and Sean Corbin for lending their emotional support, eyes, and creative opinions from the workshop birth of this book throughout the entirety of the editing phase. Love you all.

I am so grateful for my friends and family, especially the incredibly giving community of writers in Kentucky and throughout our region. There isn't a literary family anywhere like this one. Special consideration to Mom and Dad for bringing me into the world, Maurice Manning, Amanda Haan, John Lackey, JV, Chris Mattingly and Laurel, Bianca Spriggs, Matthew Haughton, my kindred spirits at Central Library, Old Red Harris for keeping me in books, local booksellers for promoting Kentucky poets, the Holler family, Accents Publishing, and Les Miller/ Al's Bar for giving poetry a home in the heart of our beautiful bluegrass home.

I would like to thank the editors of these publications where the following poems first appeared:

Still: The Journal: "plague," "Milkshake Ricky," and "silent siren"

North of Center: "Milkshake Ricky," "Have and Have-not," and "fishing for change"

The Louisville Review: "the definition of insanity"

CPSIA information can be obtained at www.ICGtesting.com
Printed in the USA
LVOW07s1316100316

478616LV00001B/41/P

9 781936 628254